I MET A PERSON ONCE

Gabriel Malca

For permission requests,
write to the author at their email address:

Author: Gabriel Malca
Email: gabriel@malca.me

ISBN: 979-8-90243-557-0

For further information about the author or their
publications,
please contact the author via email.

First Edition: 2026

A series of quiet reflections on identity, effort, and
what it means to be here.

Contents

I met a person once,
who spent a lot of time thinking about how they were being seen.

They wouldn't have described themselves that way. If you asked them, they probably would have said they were just careful. Thoughtful before they spoke. Someone who paid attention. They believed that was a good thing. A sign of maturity. Of being considerate. They weren't trying to impress anyone. They weren't chasing approval in any obvious way, at least not in a way that felt embarrassing or needy.

It was more like they were always slightly aware of themselves. Not sharply, not anxiously, just enough to stay alert. Of what they were saying. How they were saying it. Whether it sounded right. Whether it could be taken the wrong way. Whether it might create a problem later on that they would then have to deal with. The last thing they wanted was conflict, especially the kind that lingered.

They learned pretty early that things aren't always received the way you expect. That you could mean something harmless and still upset someone. That you could explain yourself clearly and still be misunderstood. And once something was out there, once it left your mouth or your screen, you couldn't really take it back. You could clarify, or apologize, or explain, but the moment itself was already gone.

So they got good at thinking things through first. Really thinking them through. Running conversations in their head before they happened. Replaying past ones afterward. Not obsessively, they would say. Just enough to learn from them. Just enough to do better next time.

They felt it most in small moments. Writing a text message or an email. Reading it back. Changing a word. Then another. Wondering if it sounded too short, like they didn't care. Or too long, like they cared too much. Wondering if the tone felt off in a way they couldn't quite put their finger on. Sometimes they erased the whole thing and started over. Sometimes they closed the app entirely and decided it wasn't worth sending after all.

And if they did send it, there it was. The waiting. That familiar tightening in their chest. Wondering how it would be read. Whether the tone came through the way they intended. Whether the other person would read something into it that wasn't there. Whether they should have added something. Or taken something out. They told themselves it didn't matter that much, but their body didn't always listen.

It wasn't just messages. It was conversations too. The pause before speaking. The moment where they weighed whether to say what they were actually thinking, or a softer version of it. The calculation that happened so quickly they barely noticed it anymore. Is this the right moment? Is this worth saying? What happens if I do?

They weren't trying to be fake. They didn't feel like they were lying. It felt more like they were managing things. Managing themselves. Keeping situations from becoming uncomfortable or messy. Making sure nothing went off the rails in a way they couldn't fix later.

They noticed how different people responded to different sides of them. Some people seemed to prefer them quieter. Some liked them helpful. Some liked them agreeable. Some liked them funny. They didn't sit down and decide to change who they were. It just happened. Over time. Like muscle memory. Like learning which version of yourself was safest in which room.

There was a version of themselves that felt acceptable to show, and another version that stayed mostly internal. The internal one wasn't dramatic or dark. It was just more direct. More opinionated. Less edited. And that version felt unpredictable. It felt like it might cause ripples they wouldn't know how to handle.

So they learned to keep certain thoughts to themselves. Certain reactions. Certain disagreements. Not forever, they told themselves. Just until the timing felt right. Just until they felt sure enough of the outcome. Just until it seemed safe to let it out without consequences.

They paid attention to reactions more than they admitted. A slower reply. A shorter answer. A shift in energy. They noticed it immediately. Even if they pretended not to. Even if they told themselves they were reading too much into it.

Sometimes they were.
Sometimes they weren't.
Either way, the noticing never really stopped.

They didn't think of themselves as anxious. They thought of themselves as aware. As someone who cared about how their actions affected others. As someone who didn't want to create problems or make situations harder than they needed to be. They believed this was just part of being an adult. Part of being decent.

People generally liked them. It reinforced the idea that the approach was working. That being measured, being careful, being easy to be around was the right way to move through the world. They weren't often rejected outright. They weren't often confronted. And that felt like success.

Still, it took effort. More than they realized at first. There was a kind of tiredness that came from always keeping track. From always checking yourself mid-moment. From never being fully inside what was happening because part of you was watching it from the outside.

There were moments when they noticed other people seemed freer somehow. Less concerned with how they sounded. Less affected by how things landed. They wondered what that felt like. To just say something and let it exist. To not replay it later. To not wonder if it had changed the way someone saw you.

They didn't sit with that thought for long. It felt impractical. Risky. Like something only certain people could afford. People who were confident. Or careless. Or protected in some way they weren't.

They told themselves they were fine the way they were. That this was just how they operated. That everyone probably did some version of this, whether they admitted it or not. And maybe they were right.

But every so often, usually when things were quiet, they noticed how much energy it took to keep themselves intact. To keep the version of themselves they presented consistent. Acceptable. Safe. How much of their attention went into not being mis-understood.

They wondered what would happen if they stopped doing that. Not all at once. Not in a dramatic way. Just a little. If they said what they meant without softening it. If they didn't correct themselves halfway through a sentence. If they didn't worry so much about how they were being received.

They also wondered what other people would think if they noticed the change.

If the people they were more honest with started talking. If someone mentioned it casually. They've been different lately. More direct. Less agreeable. The idea bothered them more than they expected.

It made them think about how the past would look in hindsight. About whether being more honest now would make it seem like they had been dishonest before. Like they had been pretending. Like all those moments of silence and agreement suddenly meant something else.

They didn't like that story.

They didn't like the idea of being seen as someone who hadn't really meant what they said. Someone who had gone along with things. Someone who had stayed quiet to avoid conflict instead of standing up for what they believed. Even if, at the time, staying quiet had felt necessary. Even if it had felt like the safest option.

They especially didn't like the idea of seeing themselves that way.

Because if they were honest, they had made choices. Not loud ones. Not obvious ones. But choices all the same. Choosing silence. Choosing agreement. Choosing to let things pass. They had told themselves it was neutral. That it kept the peace. That it didn't really matter.

At some point, it occurred to them that silence wasn't as neutral as they wanted to believe. That not speaking was still a decision. That going along with something was, in its own way, choosing a side.

That thought unsettled them.

It made everything feel heavier. More complicated. Like there was no clean way to change without questioning something. No way to be different now without looking back at who they had been.

They didn't want to open that door.

So they closed it, carefully.

They stayed busy instead. There were conversations to have. Messages to respond to. Moments to manage the way they always had. Staying measured. Staying careful. Staying familiar.

They were good at that. Very good.

Letting go of it didn't feel like freedom yet.

It felt like risk.

I met a person once,
who couldn't stop looking at where they stood compared
to everyone else.

They noticed it almost automatically. It happened when they read the news. When they scrolled past stories of people who had made it. People who seemed to live bigger lives. Lives that looked fuller, easier, more exciting. It wasn't admiration, exactly. It was more like an internal checkpoint. *Where am I in relation to this?*

They told themselves that luck played a huge role. And they probably believed that, at least intellectually. But the comparison still landed. It always did. It slipped past logic and went straight to something more sensitive.

It felt worse with people closer to them.

Someone they knew. Someone they grew up with. Someone they used to work alongside. Someone who started out in roughly the same place and somehow ended up ahead. A better job. A bigger house. More freedom. More visibility. More ease.

That was harder to explain away.

They found themselves doing the math without meaning to. What kind of salary would that require? What would their expenses be? How much help must they have had? It couldn't just be chance. It couldn't just be timing. There had to be a reason that made the difference make sense.

If they had more mouths to feed, more tuition, more expenses, that explained why they might be stretched, why their lifestyle looked a certain way. That felt fair. Balanced. Understandable.

Otherwise, the explanations had to shift. Maybe family money. Maybe connections. Maybe something behind the scenes that wasn't being talked about. Something that tipped the scale in a way that didn't feel earned. Something sketchy. That explanation hurt less than the alternative.

Because the alternative was harder to sit with.

The idea that someone out there might simply be doing better. That they might have made different choices that worked. That they might be more capable. Or more focused. Or more willing to risk things. That thought didn't feel neutral. It felt personal.

And once that feeling crept in, it brought others with it. Bitterness. Resentment. A sense that life wasn't being scored correctly. Like effort and outcome weren't lining up the way they were supposed to.

They noticed how that belief shaped their behavior. How cautious they became. How careful. Taking risks felt dangerous when you already felt behind. Losing ground felt unbearable. It was safer to protect what they had than to reach for something that might not work.

When things did go well for them, they wanted it to matter. They wanted it to register. They shared the wins. They emphasized them. They needed proof, both for themselves and for others, that they were moving forward.

Failures stayed quiet. Those were easier to manage privately. Easier to frame as temporary. Easier not to compare.

They felt this most in social situations. Being invited into someone else's life. Seeing how they lived. The size of their home. The way it was furnished. The ease with which they hosted. A beautiful space. A thoughtful meal. Effort that felt expensive, even if no one said it was.

They appreciated it. Truly. They enjoyed being there. And at the same time, something tightened.

It made them hesitate to invite that person over in return. Not because they didn't want to. But because the comparison felt unavoidable. Their own place felt smaller. Less impressive. Less put together. The idea of someone seeing that difference felt uncomfortable in a way they didn't fully understand.

So instead, they suggested dinner. A restaurant. Somewhere neutral. Somewhere no one had to open their home. No one had to cook. No one had to be seen in that way. It felt like returning the favor without having to expose anything.

That solution made sense to them. It was practical. Balanced. And yet, it subtly changed the dynamic. Something stayed uneven. Something stayed unspoken.

They didn't think of themselves as envious. They thought of themselves as realistic. They believed they were just responding to the world as it was. To numbers. To outcomes. To what could be seen.

Money made comparison easy. It was everywhere. In houses. In trips. In clothes. In experiences. In the kind of life people shared online. Carefully edited moments that looked full and exciting and happy.

They knew, logically, that money didn't equal happiness. Everyone knew that. People said it all the time. And still, it was hard not to notice how much easier life seemed to look when money was present. How success was measured through it. How quickly it became the shorthand for worth.

Character didn't show up as clearly. Kindness didn't photograph as well. Integrity didn't announce itself. Those things mattered, but they rarely led the conversation. They came second, if at all.

So the measuring continued.

No matter what they reached, there was always someone further along. Someone with more. Someone who made their progress feel smaller than it had a moment before. The bar kept moving. Quietly. Relentlessly.

And in the rare moments when they imagined stepping out of that comparison entirely, it didn't feel freeing.

It felt disorienting.

Like letting go of something that had been quietly orienting them for a long time. If they weren't measuring themselves against other people, they weren't sure how they would know if they were doing okay. Or even what "okay" was supposed to mean.

The comparison felt exhausting, but it also felt familiar. It gave them reference points. Landmarks. A sense of direction, even if that direction never really settled.

So they stayed with it.

Not because it made them happy, but because it told them where they stood.

I met a person once,
who needed to know what was coming next.

They weren't calm about it, either. Sometimes they were patient, sure. But more often than not, they were the opposite. They rushed people. They pushed for answers. They wanted decisions made now, not because they loved speed, but because waiting felt unbearable.

What they needed was clarity. A sense of direction. Some idea of how things were going to unfold so they could prepare themselves for it. The longer something stayed undefined, the louder it got in their head.

Uncertainty made them uneasy. It didn't show up as panic or fear. It just hovered. A constant background tension. When plans were vague, their mind filled in the gaps. When something was left open, they kept returning to it, running it over again and again, trying to get a handle on it.

They liked knowing the schedule. The details. The expectations. If a decision had to be made, they preferred to make it early, even if it wasn't perfect. At least then it was decided. At least then it was contained. An imperfect plan felt safer than no plan at all.

They spent a lot of time thinking ahead. Running scenarios. Imagining conversations before they happened. Preparing answers to questions that hadn't been asked yet. What if this goes wrong? What if that happens? What would I say then?

Most of the time, they didn't even notice they were doing it. Their mind just went there automatically.

It made them feel responsible. Capable. Like someone who had things under control. And control, to them, didn't feel like power. It felt like protection.

They told themselves they were just being prepared. That it was better to think things through than be caught off guard. That surprises were overrated. In their experience, surprises rarely turned out well.

They felt calmer once there was a plan. Even if it would probably change. Even if it wasn't ideal. Just knowing what was supposed to happen next brought a sense of relief. Their body relaxed a little. Their thoughts slowed down.

The opposite was also true.

When people said things like "we'll see" or "we'll figure it out," something tightened in them immediately. It sounded careless. Incomplete. Like an invitation for things to go wrong. They didn't understand how other people could be so comfortable leaving things open.

They noticed how often they took charge of situations without meaning to. Organizing plans. Handling logistics. Making decisions. Not because they wanted to control people, but because someone had to do it. And if they didn't, it might not get done properly.

It felt easier to do things themselves than to rely on someone else and risk being disappointed. That way, if something went wrong, at least they knew why. At least they could trace it back to something concrete.

They didn't think of this as controlling. They thought of it as responsible.

They liked routines. Predictability. Habits that anchored their days. Doing things in a certain order. Leaving early so they wouldn't be late. Double-checking things before they left the house. When something disrupted that rhythm, they felt it immediately.

Even randomness had to be managed somehow.

They weren't necessarily superstitious, but they had their checks. Their "just in case" habits. Leaving a little earlier than necessary. Refreshing the weather app one more time. Glancing at the clock again, even though they already knew what time it was. Doing things in a certain order because it felt wrong not to.

They didn't believe these things controlled reality. But they also didn't want to skip them. It felt safer to cover all bases than to risk finding out they should have done something differently.

Randomness felt cold.

It felt like anything could happen, for no reason at all, and you'd be left dealing with the consequences.

They preferred to believe there was some kind of order underneath things. Some logic. Some system. That actions mattered. That outcomes followed rules. That if you were careful enough, you could avoid the worst of it.

This showed up in how they related to rules and structure too. Clear guidelines were comforting. Knowing what was right and what was wrong. What was expected and what wasn't. Ambiguity made them uncomfortable. Too many options felt overwhelming.

There was comfort in systems that laid things out clearly. If you did this, this happened. If you followed the rules, you were okay. Obedience felt easier than choice. Choice came with responsibility. Responsibility came with the possibility of regret.

They didn't like regret.

They noticed how much effort it took to keep everything running smoothly. How much energy went into staying ahead of things. Anticipating problems before they happened. Making sure nothing slipped through the cracks.

Relaxing was hard. Even when nothing was wrong, part of their mind stayed alert. Watching. Monitoring. Waiting for the next thing to deal with.

They had the same dreams every so often. The kind that stuck with them all day. Being late for an exam they didn't study for. Missing a flight. Realizing they were supposed to be somewhere and weren't. Waking up with that familiar rush in their chest, even though nothing had actually happened.

Those dreams felt real. Like their body remembered something their mind didn't. Even if they'd never actually missed the exam. Even if they'd never missed the flight.

They were the ones who fell apart when plans collapsed. When a flight was canceled. When everything they had lined up suddenly unraveled. They watched other people say things like "maybe it's for the better" or "maybe something bad would have happened."

They didn't buy it.

Nothing ever blew up. No disaster was avoided. What happened was simpler than that. Lost time. Lost money. Lost opportunities they had already lived through in their head. More phone calls. More forms. More waiting. More things to fix.

It felt pointless. Wasteful. Unfair.

When they were late, it was never just lateness. It was someone else driving too slowly. Someone else missing a light. Someone else throwing off the plan. Being delayed felt personal, like something had been taken from them.

They told themselves this was just how they were wired. That it was better than being careless. Better than being unprepared. Better than being at the mercy of things they couldn't control.

And maybe they were right.

Control did reduce risk. It did prevent some mistakes. It did keep things from spiraling. Their life felt stable. Predictable. Manageable.

But it also felt tight.

They rarely felt surprised anymore. Rarely caught off guard in a good way. Spontaneity felt less like excitement and more like exposure. Like standing without armor.

When they imagined letting go of control, they didn't imagine relief. They imagined chaos. Things falling apart. People leaving. Mistakes piling up. Consequences they wouldn't be able to undo.

They didn't let that thought go very far. It felt dangerous. Like opening something they wouldn't be able to close again.

So they pulled back.

They planned more. Organized more. Checked things again. They tightened their grip in small, reasonable ways. Ways that felt justified. Necessary.

Life stayed orderly.

Nothing went terribly wrong.

And still, they were tired.

Not the tired that comes from doing too much, but the tired that comes from never fully resting. From always being a step ahead of yourself. From carrying the weight of what might happen next.

They told themselves it was the price of being responsible. Of being careful. Of keeping things together.

They didn't question it.

Not yet.

I met a person once,
who lived as if the important part came later.

They didn't think of themselves as unhappy. Busy, yes. Tired, often. But unhappy felt like the wrong word. They had direction. Momentum. Things they were working toward. That counted for something.

There was always a next step. A next goal. Something to build, improve, secure. When one thing was finished, another took its place almost immediately. It felt natural. Responsible. Like what you were supposed to do.

They told themselves they were investing in the future. Sacrificing now so things would be easier later. That story made the long days make sense. It gave meaning to the effort. It turned exhaustion into something purposeful.

They weren't reckless with their time or energy. Quite the opposite. Everything was measured. Calculated. If they were giving something up in the present, it was because it would pay off eventually. They just needed to keep going a little longer.

Rest was something they planned for, but rarely reached. It was always just ahead. After this project. After this phase. After things stabilized. There was comfort in believing that relief had a timeline, even if that timeline kept moving.

They liked progress. Numbers helped. Savings growing. Debt shrinking. Goals being checked off. It made life feel solid. Like something was accumulating. Like all this effort was turning into something tangible.

Money, especially, felt reassuring. Not because they wanted luxury, necessarily, but because it meant protection. Options. Security. It meant fewer surprises. Fewer moments where things could fall apart. They told themselves it wasn't about wanting more, it was about making sure there was enough.

Often, they framed it as responsibility toward others. Providing for their family. Their children. Making sure no one would struggle later on. That intention was real. They cared deeply. And that care justified a lot.

It justified missed moments. Long hours. Being distracted even when they were physically present. They told themselves the people they loved would understand someday. That it would all make sense once the benefits showed up.

There was always a reason to keep going.

Even their idea of enjoyment was future-oriented. Trips planned but postponed. Experiences saved for the "right time." They didn't want to enjoy things prematurely. They wanted to earn them. Pleasure felt better when it came after effort.

Sometimes, when things slowed down unexpectedly, they felt restless. Unsure what to do with the space. Without something to work toward, the days felt strangely empty. As if motion itself had become the point.

They noticed this even in how they thought about life as a whole. Not just the near future, but the far one. What they would leave behind. How they would be remembered. Whether it would all amount to something.

For some, this showed up as building. Businesses. Assets. A legacy that could be passed on. Something solid that would remain after they were gone. Proof that their time had been well spent.

For others, it showed up as careful moral accounting. Doing the right things. Following the rules. Making sure they stayed on the correct side of things. Earning favor. Earning peace. Earning whatever came next.

They didn't necessarily talk about it openly, but the thinking was there. The sense that life was being evaluated. That effort mattered beyond the moment. That there was something to be gained later, even if later wasn't clearly defined.

The present moment often felt like preparation.

They believed this was what it meant to be disciplined. To be mature. To delay gratification. To think long-term. And in many ways, it worked. Their life moved forward. Things improved. There was progress you could point to.

But the present kept shrinking.

Moments passed quickly. Conversations blurred. Joy showed up briefly and was set aside. There was always something else that needed attention. Something more important that came first.

They told themselves they would slow down eventually. When things were secure enough. When they reached a certain number. When they crossed some invisible threshold that would finally allow them to relax.

But that threshold kept shifting.

The finish line moved each time they got close. New responsibilities appeared. New risks. New reasons not to stop. The future stayed just far enough away to keep pulling them forward.

Sometimes, late at night or during rare quiet moments, they noticed how much of their life existed in anticipation. How often they were somewhere else in their mind. Somewhere ahead. Somewhere safer. Somewhere better.

They wondered what it would feel like to stop building for a moment. To not be working toward anything. To just be where they were.

The thought made them uneasy.

It felt irresponsible. Like letting go of the wheel. Like wasting time they couldn't afford to waste. So they pushed it aside and returned to what they were doing.

There was work to finish. Plans to refine. A future to secure.

Life would happen later.

I met a person once,
who didn't want to feel so much.

They wouldn't have said it that way. They didn't think of themselves as avoiding anything. They were just tired. Worn down in a way that didn't have a clear cause. The days were full, the weeks moved quickly, and by the time there was space to notice anything, they didn't really want to.

So they found ways not to.

Nothing extreme. Nothing that looked alarming from the outside. Just small things that took the edge off. Things that made the hours pass more easily. Things that helped them settle into the evening without thinking too hard about the day they'd just had.

They told themselves they deserved it. That everyone needed something to unwind. A drink. A show. Their phone. Something familiar they could sink into without effort. It wasn't about escape. It was about decompression.

At first, it worked.

The noise in their head softened. The constant pressure eased a little. The future stopped pressing so hard against the present. For a while, they could just be where they were.

They liked that feeling.

They started looking forward to it. The moment when the day finally ended and they could turn their attention elsewhere. Somewhere easier. Somewhere that didn't ask anything of them.

They didn't think of it as numbing. It felt more like relief. Like finally putting something down after carrying it for too long.

Time began to slip in strange ways. Evenings disappeared quickly. Nights stretched later than they intended. They stayed up longer than planned, not because they were having so much fun, but because stopping meant going back to themselves.

Mornings came faster than they expected.

They noticed they were more irritable during the day. Less patient. Less present. But it was manageable. Everyone was tired. Everyone was distracted. This was just how things were now.

They weren't running from anything specific. There was no single thought they were trying to avoid. It was more general than that. A vague heaviness. A low-level tension that returned whenever things got quiet.

Silence made them uneasy.

When there was nothing pulling their attention outward, their mind wandered to places they didn't want to linger. Questions with no clear answers. Feelings they didn't have time to unpack. A sense that something was off, even if they couldn't name what it was.

So they filled the space.

They checked their phone without thinking. Scrolled longer than they meant to. Let videos play one after another. Took another drink. Started another episode. Anything that kept the moment occupied.

It didn't feel compulsive. It felt normal.

They told themselves they were still functioning. Still showing up. Still doing what needed to be done. And they were. From the outside, nothing looked wrong.

But their attention was rarely fully in one place anymore. It was always split. Half in the moment, half somewhere else. Waiting for the next distraction. The next release.

They noticed how uncomfortable it felt to sit with nothing. To be alone without stimulation. Even short pauses made them restless. As if something inside them was asking for attention they didn't know how to give.

They pushed that thought away.

There would be time for that later. When things slowed down. When life was less demanding. When they weren't so tired.

For now, they just needed to get through the day.

The distractions added up quietly. Not in a way that caused problems, but in a way that dulled things. Joy felt flatter. Sadness felt heavier. Everything existed at the same low volume.

They couldn't remember the last time they felt fully absorbed in something without needing an escape afterward. Even good moments carried a kind of background fatigue.

They told themselves this was just adulthood. That everyone coped in their own way. That this was better than falling apart.

And maybe it was.

Still, every so often, usually when they caught a glimpse of themselves reflected somewhere unexpectedly, they noticed how checked out they looked. How distant. As if part of them had stepped back and stayed there.

They wondered what they were avoiding.

The question made them uncomfortable.

So they reached for something familiar and let the moment pass.

They would deal with it later.

For now, it was enough not to feel quite so much.

I met a person once,
who kept going even though they didn't know why
anymore.

From the outside, nothing had changed. They still showed up. Still handled what needed to be handled. Still moved through their days in a way that looked responsible, even productive. If you asked how they were doing, they would have said they were fine. Busy. A little tired, maybe. Nothing unusual.

But something felt different.

They noticed it in small ways at first. Things that used to give them a sense of momentum didn't land the same way. Checking things off a list felt empty. Finishing something didn't bring relief. It just led to the next thing, and the next thing felt heavier than it used to.

They kept going out of habit. Because stopping felt irresponsible. Because this was how things had always worked. You did what was in front of you. You moved forward. You didn't overthink it.

Only now, they were overthinking it anyway.

They felt tired in a way that sleep didn't fix. Even after a full night's rest, they woke up already bracing for the day. Not dreading it exactly. Just not meeting it with much of anything.

Work became mechanical. Conversations felt scripted. Even the distractions that used to help didn't work as well. They still reached for them, out of reflex, but the relief didn't last. Everything felt flatter. Muted.

They weren't unhappy. That was the confusing part. They weren't particularly sad, either. There was just less there than there used to be. Less urgency. Less excitement. Less sense that what they were doing mattered in the way it once had.

They told themselves it was burnout. Or stress. Or just a phase. Everyone went through this. Life was demanding. This was normal. It would pass.

So they pushed through.

They kept their routines. They stuck to their plans. They stayed disciplined. If anything, they doubled down on structure, hoping it would bring back a sense of control. But even that felt thin. Like going through motions that had lost their meaning.

They noticed how often they answered "Good, you?" without checking in with themselves first.

How quickly the words came out. How little space there was between the question and the response.

It wasn't a lie, exactly. It was just automatic. A way of keeping things moving. A way of not opening anything they didn't have time to deal with.

The conversation would move on, and so would they. Whatever they had been feeling stayed where it was, unnamed and unattended.

There wasn't time for it anyway. There were still responsibilities. Still people relying on them. Still things that needed to get done.

And yet, something inside them had started to resist.

They found themselves staring at screens longer than necessary. Sitting in silence without realizing how much time had passed. Feeling a strange urge to stop, even if they didn't know what stopping would look like.

Sometimes, in quiet moments, a thought would surface before they could push it away.

Why am I doing all of this?

It wasn't a dramatic question. It didn't come with panic or despair. It was almost casual. Curious, even. And that made it more unsettling.

Because they didn't have an answer ready.

They tried to replace it with the usual ones. Responsibility. Stability. The future. That's just how life works. Those answers had always been enough before. Now, they felt rehearsed. Thin.

The question lingered longer than they liked.

They noticed how easily they became irritated by small things. How patience came harder. How everything felt like effort, even things they chose. Even things they once enjoyed.

There were moments, brief and unexpected, when emotion broke through. A song. A memory. A quiet drive with no distractions. The feeling didn't last, but it left an impression. Like something underneath was still there, waiting.

They didn't know what to do with that.

So they returned to what they knew. To staying busy. To keeping things moving. To doing what made sense on paper.

They told themselves they were just tired. That this was temporary. That they didn't need to make it into something bigger.

Still, the question came back.

Not loudly. Not insistently.

Just often enough to be noticed.

They kept going.

But now, they were aware that they were doing it without knowing why.

I met a person once,
who wasn't trying to get anything from me.

T hat was what stood out right away. There was no pull in the interaction. No expectation underneath the words. They weren't waiting for me to say something useful or impressive. They didn't seem interested in where the conversation might lead or what it might turn into.

They were just there.

They didn't ask much about what I did. Not in the way people usually do, where the question is really about placing you somewhere. When I spoke, they listened, but not as if they were collecting information. There was no sense that what I said needed to be evaluated or used.

It was subtle, but it changed how I felt almost immediately.

I noticed how little effort they seemed to carry. They weren't managing the moment. They weren't filling silences. They didn't rush to respond. They let things land where they landed.

At one point, I stopped explaining myself mid-sentence. Not because I decided to, but because I realized I didn't need to. Nothing felt awkward when I did. The conversation didn't stall. Nothing needed to be fixed.

They didn't react differently. They didn't lean in or pull away. They stayed the same.

Being around them made me notice how often I feel valued for what I do, how well I do it, how smoothly I hold things together. None of that seemed to matter here. And realizing that felt strangely disarming.

There was a quiet sense of ease in it. Not excitement. Not relief. Just ease.

It reminded me of something I hadn't thought about in a long time.

When I was younger, there were moments with my family where I didn't have to explain who I was becoming yet. I didn't have to justify my choices or translate myself. I could just be there, even if everything wasn't perfect underneath.

I hadn't realized how much I still looked for that feeling.

The interaction ended the way most do. Casually. Without ceremony. We went our separate ways and I continued with my day.

But something stayed with me.

Later, doing ordinary things, I noticed myself reaching for the usual habits. Staying busy. Moving quickly from one thing to the next. Filling the space without thinking about it.

And for the first time, I noticed the effort in it.

Not in a dramatic way. Just small moments. The impulse to distract myself when there was a pause. The reflex to check something, do something, move on to the next thing instead of sitting where I was.

I hadn't questioned that before.

I didn't suddenly stop doing it. I didn't change my routine. I didn't make any decisions.

But I couldn't unsee the contrast.

For a brief moment earlier that day, I hadn't needed to be anything in particular. And now, I could feel how quickly I returned to being busy, useful, occupied.

I didn't know what that meant yet.

I only knew that something about the way I usually moved through my day had become visible to me.

And once I noticed it, it didn't disappear.

I met a person once,
who thought they had finally figured out what was wrong.

For a long time, something had felt off. Heavy. Unsettled. They couldn't point to a single cause, but the feeling followed them everywhere. And after sitting with it for a while, they reached a conclusion that made sense.

It must be their situation.

The job that drained them.

The relationship that no longer felt right.

The place that felt too small.

Once that idea took hold, everything lined up neatly. The discomfort had a source now. Something concrete they could point to. Something they could change.

Deciding to leave felt empowering. Clear. Like taking control again. For the first time in a while, there was momentum that felt hopeful instead of heavy.

They imagined how different things would feel once they were on the other side. Lighter. Freer. More aligned. The future opened up again, and that alone brought relief.

The first stretch after leaving felt good.

There was space. Distance from the old frustrations. A sense of possibility. They noticed how much better they felt not having to deal with the same problems every day.

This must have been it.

They told themselves they should have done this sooner. That they had stayed too long. That leaving was the brave choice.

But slowly, quietly, the familiar feeling returned.

Not immediately. Not all at once. Just enough to be noticed. The same restlessness. The same flatness. The same sense that something wasn't quite landing.

They tried to ignore it at first. New things take time. Adjustments come with discomfort. This was normal.

But as weeks passed, it became harder to dismiss.

They found themselves thinking about what they had left behind. Remembering it differently. The good moments grew brighter in hindsight. The problems softened around the edges.

Maybe it hadn't been that bad.

They remembered laughter. Familiar routines. The comfort of knowing what to expect. They wondered if they had been too harsh. Too impatient. Too quick to walk away.

Self-doubt crept in quietly.

They replayed conversations. Reconsidered decisions. Questioned their judgment. The narrative shifted from I needed to leave to maybe I made a mistake.

Eventually, returning felt like the responsible choice.

Going back brought relief at first. Familiar faces. Known rhythms. The sense of stepping back into something solid. It felt grounding. Safe.

And then, slowly, the original feeling resurfaced.

The same tension.

The same exhaustion.

The same sense of misalignment.

This time, it was unmistakable.

They remembered why they had left.

Not as an idea, but as a feeling. A lived experience that came rushing back once the familiarity wore off.

They hadn't been wrong.

But they also hadn't been entirely right.

What they were trying to escape hadn't lived only in the situation. And what they were looking for hadn't been waiting somewhere else.

They didn't know what the answer was yet.

They only knew that changing the outside hadn't solved what was happening inside.

And that realization stayed with them longer than the others had.

I met a person once,

who ran out of things to distract themselves with.

It didn't happen all at once. There was no clear moment where they stopped trying. They just kept reaching for the same things and noticing they didn't work the way they used to.

They picked up their phone, put it down, picked it up again. Scrolled without really seeing anything. Opened apps out of habit. Closed them just as quickly.

They tried staying busy. Cleaning things that didn't need cleaning. Organizing drawers. Making lists they didn't intend to follow. Anything that gave the feeling of doing something.

When that didn't help, they told themselves this was just life. That this was what adulthood felt like. That everyone felt bored, tired, unmotivated sometimes. You accepted it and moved on.

Acceptance felt easier than sitting with whatever this was.

They told themselves a story about the cards they'd been dealt. About how some people just had more energy. More excitement. More luck. This was simply how things were for them.

That explanation gave them something to lean on. A way to stop questioning.

Still, the discomfort stayed.

They noticed how restless they felt when there was nothing to do. How quickly they looked for noise. For movement. For something to occupy the space. Silence felt too open. Like something might slip in if they weren't careful.

At one point, they sat down without meaning to. Not as a decision. Just because there was nowhere else to go.

They stayed there longer than they planned.

At first, it was uncomfortable. Their mind jumped around. They thought about things they should be doing. Things they hadn't done. Things they could do next. The familiar urge to get up came quickly.

But for a brief moment, they didn't.

Nothing dramatic happened.

The world didn't collapse.

Nothing rushed in to overwhelm them.

They didn't fall apart.

There was just a feeling. Subtle. Hard to describe. Not peace. Not clarity. Just a sense of being here without trying to manage it.

It passed quickly.

Almost immediately, the urge to move returned. To do something. To fill the space again. And they did. They stood up. Picked something up. Continued on.

But that small moment stayed with them.

Not because it was profound, but because it contradicted something they believed. The idea that if they stopped, everything would fall apart. That boredom or stillness was dangerous. That there was nothing on the other side of it.

They hadn't discovered anything new.

But they had discovered that nothing terrible happened.

And that was enough to make the discomfort feel slightly less threatening.

I met a person once,
who hesitated before filling the space.

It wasn't intentional at first. More like a pause where a habit usually lived. The urge to reach for something was there, familiar and automatic. They noticed it, waited a second, and didn't act on it right away.

That alone felt strange.

They weren't trying to be present. They weren't experimenting. They just didn't move as quickly as they normally did. The moment stretched slightly, and they stayed in it.

Their mind reacted immediately. A rush of thoughts. Things they should be doing. Reasons this was a waste of time. A low-level anxiety that came with not being occupied.

They almost stood up.

But they didn't.

The feeling underneath wasn't calm. It was exposed. Like standing in a room without furniture. There was nothing to lean on. No structure to hide behind. Just themselves, unbuffered.

They felt the urge to explain it away. To turn it into something productive. I'm just resting. I deserve a break. This is probably healthy. The mind wanted a frame.

They didn't give it one.

They noticed sensations instead. Tightness in their chest. A shallow breath. Restlessness in their body. Things they usually drowned out with movement or noise.

None of it was overwhelming. It was just unfamiliar.

The longer they stayed, the more they noticed how quickly the urge to escape returned. To check something. To do something. To re-enter motion.

They let themselves leave when it got uncomfortable.

They didn't push through.

Later, they noticed something subtle.

The pause hadn't fixed anything. It hadn't made them feel better. But it had changed the texture of the day. They felt slightly less compelled to fill every gap. Slightly more aware of the moment before the reflex kicked in.

They didn't do it consistently. Sometimes they forgot entirely. Other times they noticed and chose distraction anyway.

But occasionally, they hesitated.

And in that hesitation, they realized something small but important.

They didn't need to know what would happen next in order to stay for a moment.

They weren't safe yet.

They weren't settled.

They weren't at peace.

But they were present enough to notice when they were about to disappear.

And for now, that was as far as they were willing to go.

I met a person once,
who stopped long enough to let themselves feel.

They didn't plan to. There was no intention behind it. They were just tired of running from one thing to the next, tired of filling every gap the moment it appeared. So when a pause showed up, they didn't immediately rush past it.

They stayed.

At first, nothing happened. And that almost felt like relief. Like maybe all the discomfort they'd been avoiding was exaggerated. Maybe there was nothing underneath it after all.

Then a feeling surfaced.

Not sharp. Not dramatic. Just present. A heaviness they hadn't noticed carrying until they stopped moving. It didn't seem connected to what was happening around them. There was no clear reason for it to be there.

They waited for it to get worse.

They expected it to swell, to overwhelm them, to prove why staying still had always felt dangerous. That's what they'd imagined would happen if they ever stopped long enough. That everything they'd been holding back would come rushing in all at once.

But it didn't.

The feeling came in waves. It rose, lingered, softened. Then something else followed. Not in order. Not cleanly. A flicker of sadness. A tension in the chest. A quiet ache they couldn't quite name.

Their mind immediately tried to get involved.

Where is this coming from?

Why now?

This doesn't make sense.

They searched for an explanation. A memory. A recent event. Something they could point to and say, that's it. But nothing fit neatly. The feelings felt older than that. Less specific.

It dawned on them that these weren't new emotions at all.

They were familiar. Buried. Things they had learned, slowly, to step around. To push aside. To smooth over. Not consciously. Just by staying busy. By staying forward-facing. By not lingering.

Their mind had done its job well.

As the feelings moved through them, something else became noticeable. Underneath the emotion, beneath the discomfort, there was something quieter. Something vulnerable. A sense of presence that didn't come with words.

It felt oddly familiar.

Not like discovering something new, but like remembering something they'd known before and lost track of. A version of themselves that existed before all the managing. Before all the layers.

This wasn't a thought. It wasn't an insight. It was a feeling of being here, without armor.

That realization unsettled them more than the emotions had.

Because if this was them — if this was what had been underneath the walls and routines and plans — then what had they been protecting all this time?

They felt exposed. Uncontrolled. Like they had stepped outside of the identity they'd built. The one that knew how to function. How to cope. How to stay intact.

They didn't trust it.

The lack of control scared them. The fact that they couldn't predict what would come next. The fact that they couldn't manage it with thinking or effort.

They worried that if they stayed here too long, they would lose something important. Their edge. Their clarity. The version of themselves that knew how to survive.

So they didn't stay long.

They let the moment pass. Got up. Returned to their day. Slipped back into familiar rhythms. The thinking mind resumed its place. Planning. Organizing. Managing.

Life went on.

Nothing fell apart.

And that surprised them.

Over the next few days, everything looked the same from the outside. Same responsibilities. Same routines. Same distractions. But something had shifted internally.

They noticed how quickly they reached for noise now. How reflexive it was. How automatic the avoidance felt. They hadn't noticed it before.

They also noticed something else.

They missed that moment.

Not the discomfort. Not the uncertainty. But the feeling of touching something real. Of being closer to themselves than they usually allowed.

They didn't know how to get back there intentionally. And part of them didn't want to. It still felt risky. Uncontained.

But another part remembered.

It remembered that the emotions hadn't destroyed them. That the lack of control hadn't erased them.

That underneath everything they'd built, there was something alive. Something that didn't need to be managed to exist.

They weren't ready to live from that place.

They weren't ready to trust it.

But now they knew it was there.

And once you've felt yourself, even briefly, it becomes harder to believe that staying numb is the same as being safe.

I met a person once,
who didn't know where they belonged anymore.

After realizing they could pause without falling apart, they started doing it more often. Not for long. Just a few extra seconds here and there. Enough to feel something underneath the noise.

They didn't talk about it. They didn't announce anything. They were careful not to make it a big deal. They still remembered the kinds of people they used to roll their eyes at. The ones who suddenly had answers. The ones who made everything sound profound.

They didn't want to become that.

So they approached it quietly. Carefully. Reading a little. Watching a video or two. Trying yoga once. Sitting still occasionally and calling it "stretching" or "rest" instead of anything more loaded.

They wanted to understand what was happening without drifting too far from who they had been.

But something had already shifted.

They started noticing things they hadn't before. The way conversations followed predictable paths. How often people talked without really listening. How much energy went into posturing, signaling, proving.

They had been part of it. They knew the rhythm. The rules. The unspoken agreements. Before, it had all felt normal. Necessary, even.

Now it felt louder.

The pursuit of things that once felt essential didn't land the same way. Money still mattered, but it no longer felt like the measure of everything. Status felt fragile. Friendships built entirely around convenience or shared distraction felt thinner.

They didn't judge it. They just noticed the distance growing.

At times, they felt like an outsider. Still present, still participating, but not fully inside it anymore. Like watching a game they used to play, suddenly aware of the rules instead of absorbed in them.

That awareness was unsettling.

They missed the simplicity of believing in it all without question. Of knowing where they stood. Of having clear markers for success, progress, belonging.

Without those, things felt undefined.

They felt the pull to replace what they'd lost. To anchor themselves to something new. A framework. A label. A way to explain who they were becoming.

They thought about calling it growth. Or awareness. Or consciousness. They tested the words
quietly, to themselves. None of them fit quite right.

The thing they had touched didn't feel like an
identity. It didn't ask to be named. It didn't give them
a role to step into.

And that made it hard to hold.

Humans need something to belong to. A story
that says, *this is who I am*. Without that, there's a kind
of floating. A sense of being unmoored.

They tried to hold on to the feeling instead. To
return to it. To recreate it. To stay connected to
whatever had opened up inside them.

But the more they tried to grasp it, the further
away it felt.

It wasn't something they could perform. Or
maintain. Or live from full-time. It didn't replace the
old structures with new ones. It simply existed,
quietly, underneath everything else.

Some days, they felt closer to it. Other days,
completely disconnected. They worried they were
losing it. That they were slipping back into old
patterns and missing their chance.

That fear made them tense. Made them watch
themselves too closely. Made them question every
decision. *Is this aligned? Is this real? Am I betraying
something?*

It was exhausting.

Eventually, they noticed something important.

The moments where they felt most connected weren't the ones where they tried hardest. They were the moments where they stopped trying to define themselves at all.

Moments where they were just present. Ordinary. Unremarkable. Without needing to belong to anything in particular.

That was uncomfortable in its own way.

But it was also honest.

They didn't know how to live from that place yet.

And maybe they didn't need to.

For now, they were learning something quieter.

They didn't have to replace one identity with another.
They didn't have to explain themselves.
They didn't have to belong to anything yet.

They could just be.

And slowly, that began to feel less like losing themselves
and more like leaving room for something real to stay.

I met a person once,
who thought they had finally figured it out.

After touching something real, they wanted to understand it. And understanding led them somewhere familiar. Books. Talks. Podcasts. Teachers who spoke with confidence about things they themselves could barely put into words yet.

They listened carefully. Took notes. Highlighted passages that resonated. Certain ideas made sense immediately. They fit what the person had felt in their own body. That felt validating.

It was comforting to hear someone else explain it so clearly.

They still approached it logically. They didn't accept everything blindly. They agreed with what aligned. What felt true. What matched their experience so far. That made it feel grounded. Reasonable.

Slowly, a framework formed.

They began seeing patterns everywhere. In conversations. In behavior. In the way people chased things that no longer seemed important. Status. Money. Approval. Noise.

They had been there too. Not long ago.

That realization created distance.

They noticed how unaware other people seemed. How caught up. How reactive. How unwilling to pause. It was hard not to see it once they had.

At first, the noticing felt neutral. Observational.

Then it started to feel frustrating.

Why couldn't others see it?
Why did people keep repeating the same mistakes?
Why did they resist something that felt so obvious now?

They wanted to help.

They shared insights carefully at first. Dropping comments. Asking questions. Suggesting books. Pointing things out gently. Sometimes people listened. Sometimes they didn't.

When they didn't, it stung more than expected.

They told themselves they were only trying to help. That they wished someone had told them sooner. That they were saving people time, pain, unnecessary suffering.

But underneath that was something else.

Impatience.

They had crossed a line they couldn't unsee, and now they expected others to cross it too. When they didn't, it felt personal. Like resistance. Like refusal.

They didn't notice how quickly certainty had replaced curiosity.

They judged reactions. Labeled people as asleep or aware. Closed or open. In denial or on the path. They didn't say it out loud, but they felt it.

They had traded one identity for another.

Before, they were part of the noise.
Now, they were outside of it.

That felt important.

They hadn't yet realized how new this understanding was. How fragile. How partial. They spoke about truth without being able to define it. About faith without trusting it. About surrender while still expecting outcomes.

They read that life was happening *for* them, not *to* them. They liked that idea. It made sense.

Until something didn't go the way they thought it should.

A setback. A loss. A missed opportunity. Something that didn't bend toward their understanding.

They felt confused. Then frustrated.

If life was happening for them, why did this feel so wrong?
Why did it hurt?
Why didn't it align?

They noticed how quickly they wanted meaning to justify the outcome. How uncomfortable it was to sit with the possibility that they didn't know. That they couldn't see far enough ahead to understand what this was serving.

They had believed faith meant knowing everything would work out a certain way.

They hadn't yet learned that faith often means **not knowing,** and not demanding that reality explain itself on your timeline.

They were still trying to control the unfolding — just with better language.

Helping others became exhausting. Watching people regress after moments of clarity felt defeating. They took it personally when advice wasn't followed. When insights weren't integrated. When change didn't stick.

They didn't yet see that understanding cannot be transferred. That timing matters. That no one can be dragged into awareness without resistance.

They were learning that the hard way.

Eventually, the frustration caught up with them.

They were tired of explaining. Tired of correcting. Tired of carrying a truth that didn't feel as solid as they pretended it was.

Somewhere in that exhaustion, something softened.

They began noticing how little they actually knew. How small their window really was. How quickly certainty had turned into another kind of armor.

They started speaking less.

Listening more.

Not because they had reached humility, but because the effort of being right had worn them down.

They hadn't lost what they'd found.

But they were beginning to see that real understanding doesn't need to announce itself.

And that faith, whatever it was, didn't ask life to bend toward their will.

It asked them to loosen their grip.

I met a person once,
*who stopped forcing themselves into places they no longer
fit.*

I t didn't happen dramatically. There was no announcement. No decision to cut people off or redraw their life all at once. They simply started noticing how certain things felt in their body.

Some invitations landed differently now. Conversations that once felt familiar began to feel draining halfway through. Certain dynamics left them tense in a way they could no longer ignore.

Before, they would have pushed past that. Told themselves it wasn't a big deal. That being agreeable was easier than making things awkward. That saying yes was just part of being a good person.

Now, the signal was harder to override.

They noticed it when they said yes out of habit and felt it immediately. A tightness. A heaviness. A quiet resistance that didn't go away with logic. And they noticed how different it felt when they didn't explain themselves.

"I can't make it."
"I'm not up for that."
"This doesn't feel right for me anymore."

They didn't follow it with reasons. They didn't soften it to be more acceptable. They didn't rush to reassure the other person.

To their surprise, the world didn't collapse.

Some people pushed back. Some didn't understand. A few drifted away. And others adjusted without much fuss at all.

They were learning that boundaries didn't require defense. Only clarity.

As they moved through their days this way, old relationships began to change shape. Some grew quieter. Some faded entirely. Not out of anger, but out of honesty.

There had been resentment earlier in the journey. Toward people who hadn't shown up. Toward dynamics that felt one-sided. Toward versions of themselves that had stayed too long.

That resentment had been loud at first. Sharp. Protective.

Over time, it softened.

Not because the past was rewritten, but because it was understood differently. They began to see how those relationships had met them where they were. How they had served a purpose at a certain stage. How both sides had been doing the best they could with what they had.

Some connections weren't meant to last forever. They were meant to guide. To challenge. To reflect something that needed to be seen.

Once that work was done, there was no need to keep dragging them forward.

Letting go didn't feel like loss anymore. It felt like completion.

There was gratitude in that. Quiet, unspoken gratitude. For what had been learned. For what had been survived. For what no longer needed to be repeated.

They noticed how different their energy felt now in the presence of others. Less porous. Less entangled. Not closed off, but contained.

They didn't absorb everything anymore. Other people's moods didn't stick the way they used to. Expectations didn't automatically become obligations.

It wasn't armor.
It wasn't withdrawal.

It was discernment.

They still cared deeply. Still showed up when it felt right. Still loved without holding on too tightly.

But they no longer abandoned themselves to maintain connection.

There was a sense of trust in this. Trust in their ability to feel what was right and wrong for them without needing to justify it. Trust that what belonged in their life would remain without force.

They weren't isolating.

They were making room.

Room for relationships that could meet them where they were now. Room for conversations that didn't require performance. Room for a life that didn't need constant negotiation.

They didn't feel superior. If anything, they felt more ordinary. More human.

They had stopped trying to be everything for everyone.

And in doing so, they became more available to what was actually theirs to carry.

I met a person once,
*who returned to their life without trying to make it mean
something.*

There was no clear line between before and after. No moment they could point to and say, *this is where everything changed.* Things looked mostly the same from the outside.

They still woke up to the same days. Still handled the same responsibilities. Still moved through familiar spaces.

What had changed was quieter.

They no longer felt the need to explain themselves as much. Or justify their choices. Or translate their inner experience into something that made sense to everyone else.

When something didn't feel right, they noticed it sooner. When something felt true, they trusted it without needing to convince anyone.

They listened more than they spoke. And when they did speak, it wasn't to persuade or correct. It was simply to respond.

They didn't rush to fill silence. They didn't rush to offer advice. They didn't rush to fix what wasn't asking to be fixed.

They noticed how often life invited presence without ceremony. A conversation that didn't need direction. A moment that didn't need improvement. A feeling that didn't need to be named.

They let those moments be enough.

They still cared deeply. Still hoped. Still felt disappointment when things didn't go as expected. But they no longer argued with reality when it didn't align with their understanding.

They met it where it was.

Old patterns showed up from time to time. The urge to control. To measure. To return to certainty. They noticed those too, without panic.

They didn't see them as failures.

Just reminders.

There was less effort now. Less striving to be someone. Less urgency to arrive anywhere else.

They trusted that what needed to move would move. And what stayed would stay without force.

They didn't feel special. If anything, they felt more ordinary than before.

And that felt right.

They had stopped searching for themselves in ideas, roles, or futures. They were no longer waiting to become something else.

They were here.

And for the first time in a long while, that was enough.